I0004025

# A DAILY ROUTINE CAN TRANSFORM YOUR LIFE

## SIMBLE T ASHOKAN

All those who want to get organised and achieve their goal.

# Contents

# Acknowledgements

Writing this book has been more rewarding than I could have ever imagined. None of this would have been possible without the love and support from my family who inspired me at different stages of my journey. I would like to honor and respect my grandparents. I am grateful to my parents who believed in me and gave me the freedom to choose and my son Ivaan and daughter Ivaaniya for their unconditional love and support that shaped me. I thank my sister Ambily Vinod for her love and prayers and her daughters Avinbala and Krishnabala. I would like to thank my mentors for helping me find my true calling in life. Without them, I would have never known my true potential as a personal coach. Last but not the least, My heartfelt gratitude to all my clients all over the world. None of this would be possible without a great group of individuals-the members of my Life Architects Hub. I love you all and I wake up each day looking forward to nurturing this group. I have got help from not just these names, but hundreds of others. The journey of writing this book is not a one-man journey. I am thankful to RoseRani & Shabeena. They are my true friends. Once again, I would like to acknowledge every single person who has inspired me on this journey.

# 1
# INTRODUCTION

———•♡•———

A day is all we have to live on, what do we do with our time? You may be a student, a professional, homemaker, a retired person or a person working from home. We do have to make a conscious decision and choices on how we spend our time. It determines our happiness, peace of mind, career success, health, harmony in relationships, financial freedom and fulfilment in life. You can either waste a day or use it for your best. This makes me want to write a book about how we can create our own daily routine to make our dreams a reality.

I don't believe in writing a big book with lots of information. But I strongly believe in small simple actions which give results in our life rather than gathering information. Therefore, I keep my book short, practical and actionable. In this book, I share some of my ideas on how to build a daily routine for yourself. If you feel you are always busy but have no results, it's the right time for you to build a perfect daily routine that works for you.

# 2

# WHY SHOULD YOU CREATE A DAILY ROUTINE?

Are you a person with goals in your life?

When will you achieve this goal?

What is your life goal?

Writedown your 10years , 5years, 3 years, 1 year goals in each area of your life below or in a separate notebook.

Career Goal

1

2

3

4

5

Health Goal

1

2

3

4

5

Wealth Goal

1

2

3

4

5

Relationship Goal

1

2

3

4

5

Charity Goal

1

2

3

4

5

Now you have the clarity about your goals to achieve within 10 years,5 years,3 years & in one year. You can divide your one-year goal in to 12 small pieces of monthly goals. From each monthly goals, determine your weekly goals. From each weekly goals, you can set your daily goals. Now it is clear what is the importance of building a perfect daily routine to achieve your goal.

Do you feel stressed out during the day with all the tasks you have to do? Do you feel like you have no idea about how to get everything done?

Successful people are known to have a daily routine. Daily habits may vary depending on a person. They may include such things as meditation, exercise, and reading a book. These small activities form a system according to which we all function. And such a system determines our success both at personal and professional life. Creating a daily routine is going to change your life!

# 3
# BENEFITS OF BUILDING A PERFECT DAILY ROUTINE

1. Establishing a daily routine is both a self-investment and a way to do your best for the world.
2. When you have a specific plan for the day, week or even month, it's easier to achieve your goals.
3. It helps to keep order in life. You will feel much more organized and confident in yourself.
4. Following a daily routine can help you establish priorities, better time management, self-discipline.
5. It helps you to understand yourself better, keep track of goals, and even make you healthier.
6. Daily habits easily eliminate distractions because you are focused only on those things that need to be done.
7. It allows you to reorganize your schedule and adjust to possible changes.
8. The less you are thinking about all the things you need to do, the less stress you will have! Reduce your anxiety for the day ahead. You will be more productive to fulfil your life.

# 4

# WHAT'S A PERFECT DAILY ROUTINE?

There isn't a fixed daily routine that will work for everyone. What works for someone else, might not work for you. Finding the perfect daily routine for you is a process that involves a lot of trial and error. It all depends on you.

Once you achieve that, the routine becomes something natural and you'll do everything automatically. You can create a perfect daily routine according to your needs and wants. It can also contribute to your personal and professional success.

# 5

# HOW CAN YOU PLAN YOUR DAILY ROUTINE?

———♡———

Planning is the key to having a fulfilled life. There is so much freedom in planning. You can get to your dream destination more quickly if you plan for it. When you are planning your daily routine, take into account other affecting variables like if you have kids, the time you wake up, your work nature and so on. You can personalize your daily routine accordingly.

If you do not have a routine, can we create one?

The first step is to look into what you need to do daily. Make a list of all those tasks and group them into five categories.

The categories are given below.

### *YOURSELVES.*

1.

### *FAMILY.*

2.

### *CAREER.*

3.

## *FINANCIAL FREEDOM.*

4.

## *SPIRITUAL OR FOR OTHERS.*

Let's see examples for each category.

**1) What do you do to make you happy & for your health (physical, mental & emotional health).**

- Examples:
- Meditation
- prayer
- exercise
- healthy food
- water consumption
- spiritual study
- self-reflection
- gratitude journal
- goal writing
- hobby
- forgiveness practice
- sleeping etc.

**2) What do you do for family? Prepare a list of activities for a harmonious loving family.**

Examples:

- Make sure to spend some quality time with family without distractions (mobile).

You can plan some activities with family members like

- Prayer
- Meal time

- A small vacation
- Get together
- Shopping
- Meditation
- Exercise
- Organise home (cleaning, washing)
- Evening walk
- Play with kids
- Help children in their study time.

### 3)What do you do for career success?
Examples: -

- Learn something new
- Make use of your travelling time to the office to listen to podcasts or audio books.
- Plan & organise work schedule.
- Take necessary training to enhance your skills and talents
- Join a new course which helps your career growth.
- You can do reflection on your career and check can you utilise your skills and talents, or is it time to your change career? Take action.

### 4) What do you do for financial freedom

- Do financial audit (write down your income, expense)
- Learn personal finance management.

### 5)What do we do to support others?
What are all we do for others? Prepare your list. Do something that makes others happy. Develop love and compassion for others, it actually makes you happy.

- Do some social work.
- Do some charity.

· You can help others with money or give a beautiful smile or kind words.

Do what you can.

## *ACTION PLAN FOR YOU: -*

Prepare a list of tasks or activities for the above five areas.

Now you got all your daily tasks ready. We can divide 24 hours into four blocks. Take your daily tasks one by one and put it into suitable blocks. So, determine first which task comes under which block.

## BLOCK 1- Morning Schedule

## BLOCK 2- Work Schedule

## BLOCK 3- Evening Schedule

## BLOCK 4- Night Schedule

Starting with the most important, non-negotiable tasks, add each task into each block, making sure that each task actually fits.

Don't try to do it all at once. Start including one thing or two and see how that works for you. If possible, try to give yourself extra time for each task as you add it to each block. If you find these new schedule works and you still have time for other things, you may include them as well. Slowly, adapt and change your routine little by little until it completely satisfies you.

## BLOCK1: -MORNING SCHEDULE

How you start your day determines how it finishes. As we start each day fresh, we can better focus on what is in front of us, where to prioritize our time, and, ultimately, increase our productivity. I love studying the habits of successful people because I believe their habits play a major role in their success. If successful people find time from their busy schedules for morning routines, why don't you find some time for yourself in the morning for selfcare?

Morning routines can be as long as 1 hour or as short as 5-6 minutes. So, lack of time is never an excuse to skip your morning routine. When you are starting out, you can start small. But you must build it up to at least one hour so that you can truly benefit from it. The same daily morning routine isn't something that applies to all. However, there are certain activities that are recommended by professionals, and successful people.

## WAKE UP EARLY

If you are consistent with your sleeping habits, you can find out time for your morning routine.

## PRACTICE GRATITUDE

Appreciate the fact that you are alive and appreciate everything that you have. Think of three things that you are grateful for.

## HYDRATE

After 7 to 8 hours of sleep, your body is dehydrated. A dehydrated body doesn't perform well. So, drink a glass or two of water in the morning.

## MEDITATE

Before getting involved in busy schedules, take time to meditate, to calm your mind. Meditation helps in making important decisions in a proactive state than in a reactive state.

## MOVE AROUND

Either walk, exercise, or stretch while making breakfast. Your body loves movement and being active since the morning prepares you to be active for the rest of the day.

## VISUALIZATION

Simply close your eyes and imagine yourself excelling and being the best you. Put yourself in situations where you shine, visualizing the best possible outcome. Include as much detail in your visualizations as possible, using all of your senses.

## MAKE A DAILY TO-DO LIST

One great way to be fully prepared for the day ahead is to make a to-do list. When planning your day, identify your top 3 to-do's. These are the tasks that if you complete, you will feel satisfied with your day – no matter what.

## LEARN SOMETHING NEW

Keep aside 30 minutes a day for learning. There is no saturation point when it comes to education. Spend your time learning new and improving your skills.

## SPEND TIME THINKING

Most people do not spend time thinking about what they could do better. Spend 15 minutes a day thinking, "What can I do better? "You can improve your life in any area if you take the time to think. During the allocated minutes, you can generate new ideas, fix current problems. Keep track of the thoughts. You can also use the time to identify your mistakes and achievements. List them down and analyse every single one. Thinking is one of your most powerful abilities. Use it

## *ACTION PLAN FOR YOU*

What are all you going to include in your block 1, morning schedule?

Prepare a list of morning tasks and the time needed to complete each task. Examples-

- Meditation 20 minutes,
- Exercise 20 minutes
- Cooking 2-hour,
- Breakfast 15 minutes,
- School preparation 10 minutes,
- Get ready to the office in 15 minutes etc.

## BLOCK 2: - WORK SCHEDULE

If you travel half an hour to reach your office, you have an opportunity to use it to your advantage. An hour of travel a day, summed up for five working days, adds up to 20 hours a month.

You can use your travelling time to listen to a podcast, take up an audio-based course, or digest an audiobook. If you do not drive to work, you can use the time to do easy tasks such as making some pending calls, thinking how you could make your day productive, how your day went by, and more.

When you have ten tasks to complete, working in time slots helps you make progress towards all of them. If you work on one task, wait to finish it and then move on to the next, then some tasks may be in pending state. Instead, make a work schedule for yourself. Set a time slot for each task. You can decide the time allowed before starting the task. If you overshoot the timeline, leave the task pending and move on to the next one. If time permits at the end of all tasks, you can come back to what you left behind. Make a rough mental estimate on what is the maximum time you should spend on the task. You can also allow a specific amount of time for a project you procrastinate regularly.

- Work on one thing at a time.
- Avoid unnecessary meetings.
- Make it a habit to decline meetings that you feel are a waste of time.
- Take breaks during work, preferably after every hour.

## *ACTION PLAN FOR YOU*

Prepare your work schedule according to your work nature.

## BLOCK 3: - EVENING SCHEDULE

Evenings are a time to relax and a good evening routine gives you a chance to reflect, refresh and recharge. Spend some quality time with yourself and family.
Some examples are given below.

- Go for a walk-in nature
- Gardening
- Hobby
- Putting on some music or watching your favourite show.
- Taking a nap.
- Do something that you love.

Reflection is an important part of life that a lot of us can neglect. There are many ways in which you can reflect. The best way is to journal.

- Prepare for tomorrow.
- Decluttering the house
- Laying out clothes
- Cooking.

## *ACTION PLAN FOR YOU*

Take a book and pen and now it's your time to prepare your evening activities and the time taken to complete.

## BLOCK 4: - NIGHT ROUTINE

Developing a good night routine before bed can help you a lot with sleeping and preparing yourself for the next day.
**Why is sleep so important?**
Sleep is vital to your health, both mentally and physically. A sound sleep helps the body and mind repair itself. It also repairs your brain at night. When you lack sleep, it's harder for you to learn, make decisions and solve problems.
**How will a bedtime routine help me?**
If you have trouble sleeping, a healthy bedtime routine can make all the difference. A routine offers repetition, which will help your body recognize that you're getting ready to sleep. It will help your body start the wind-down process.

## *YOUR SPACE CLEAN*

Physical clutter equals mental clutter. Going around your home before bed and putting things where they belong is going to make a big difference in how your home looks and feels.

## *WRITE DOWN 3 GOOD THINGS ABOUT YOUR DAY*

Expressing gratitude towards the good things in your life is the key to a happy mindset. A good practice is to write down 3 good things that happened to you that day.

## TURN OFF THE TECH

Turn off the cell phones, tablets and computers before you go to bed. When it gets dark, your body starts to produce melatonin to help you prepare for sleep. But the bright which slows down the melatonin production and makes it harder to sleep.

## READING OR WRITING IN THE HOUR BEFORE BED

It helps your body wind down and shift into sleep mode. Try journaling before bed

## WRITE DOWN A TO-DO LIST

While you're writing, think about writing down a to-do list for the next day. It can help clear your mind and help take away some of those anxieties about tomorrow before bed.

TAKING A WARM BATH.

It helps relax and loosen your muscles, which helps prepare your body for sleep

DEEP BREATHING HELP YOU TO FALL ASLEEP.

It makes you feel calm, relaxes your muscles and slows your heart rate. Those are all important in helping you sleep at night.

## SLEEPING TIME

Decide your sleeping time. Example 10PM to 5AM.

## WEEKLY ROUTINE

Weekly schedule completely depends on you. Pick a day of the week that works best for you and stick to it. Weekends are meant to relax. As nothing in excess is ever good, schedule time for social gatherings, movies, hobbies and planning for the week ahead.

- Use some of your weekend time learning the skills of the job you want.
- Decluttering your living spaces will make you feel better, especially if you can give some of those items to charity, or sell them online.
- Meal planning, grocery shopping, and then preparing meals is a process. But if you start a week without a plan, everything fails. Given enough time to choose meals as well as plan your shopping list. Post your meal plan posted where you can see it.
- You can plan for a deep home cleaning
- You can plan for your self-care
- Give yourselves a break.
- Take some time to reflect on the week gone by. Reflection is something you should be doing daily, but weekends are a great time to appreciate what you have and reflect on your happiness and accomplishments, what you're grateful for and how to make the next week even better.
- Make some quality time for family and friends.This is important for those who don't spend much time with their loved ones during the week.
- Painting/Gardening/crafts/exercise/cooking/cultural activities.This is important for those who are in an office all week.

## ACTION PLAN FOR YOU

Prepare your weekend schedule according to your needs and goals.

# 6

# HOW TO CREATE A PERFECT DAILY ROUTINE FOR OURSELVES

———————♡———————

Are you ready to create your daily routine?

Yes. Find out some time to create one that works for you.

Take a book and pen.

To make a better daily routine, start by making a list of all your tasks. Think of everything, including the little things, that you do on a daily basis. Are there any tasks that you only do on certain days? Make sure to list those, too! Once you have a list of everything you need to accomplish, make a note of the amount of time that each task takes, like 10minutes or an hour. Then, prioritize each activity.

Categorise your tasks into five categories.

**1)FOR YOURSELVES: - List out all the tasks, you do for your happiness, health etc**

    1............................

    2............................

    3............................

    4............................

5.............................

**2)FOR YOUR FAMILY: -List out all tasks you do for your family.**

1.............................

2.............................

3.............................

4.............................

5.............................

**3)FOR YOUR CAREER: -List out all tasks you do for career success.**

1.............................

2.............................

3.............................

4.............................

5.............................

**4)FOR YOUR FINANCIAL FREEDOM: -List out what do you do for personal finance management**

1.............................

2.............................

3.............................

4.............................

5.............................

**5)FOR CHARITY OR FOR OTHERS: -List out all activities to help others.**

1.............................

2.............................

3.............................

4.............................

5.............................

Have you completed it? Now you have all your daily tasks almost in all areas and can put all tasks into four blocks. So, determine which task comes under which block.

Suppose you are a person who gets up in the morning at 5AM, goes to work at 8.30AM, comes by 5.30PM and sleeps at night at 10PM.

Your block 1, morning schedule is [5AM-8.30AM]

Your block 2, work schedule is [8.30AM-5.30PM]

Your block 3, evening schedule is[5.30PM-9PM]

Your block 4, night Routine is [9PM-10PM]

The above schedule is for example. You can make changes according to your needs and goals.

Now it's time to put your daily tasks to each block.

**BLOCK1-MORNING SCHEDULE**

1......................................

2......................................

3......................................

4......................................

5......................................

1.Meditation – [5AM-5.20AM]

2.Exercise –[5.20AM-5.40AM]

3.Shower-[5.40AM-6.00AM]

4.Cooking-[6AM-8AM]

5.Breakfast-[8AM-8.15AM]

6.Get ready to office-[8.15AM-8.30AM]

The above is for example. You can prepare and change for your goal.

**BLOCK2-WORK SCHEDULE**

1......................................

2......................................

3......................................

4......................................

5......................................

For example

1.Travel time to the office. Listen to podcasts/audio books [8.30AM-9AM].

2.Work time [9AM-5PM]

**BLOCK3-EVENING SCHEDULE**

1......................................

2......................................

3......................................

4......................................

5..........................................

For Example,

1.Refresh and relax with family[5.30PM-6PM]

2.Watch social media/Gardening[6PM-6.30PM]

**BLOCK4-NIGHT SCHEDULE**

1..........................................

2..........................................

3..........................................

4..........................................

5..........................................

**ACTION PLAN**

Write down your daily routine. Prepare it in a table. You can take a printout of this and can paste it on your wall.

# 7

# TEST-DRIVE YOUR NEW ROUTINE

Once everything is all set up, it's time to practice the routine and test-drive it for 30 days. Once your schedule is written, try it out for a few days and make sure it works for you. After you've followed your routine for a few days, ask yourself these questions to make sure you've created your perfect daily routine:

Is your routine realistic?

Do you have enough time to complete each task?

Does your routine make sense, or should you try the activities in a different order?

If you need to do some tasks only on certain days, create several versions of your daily routine. You can make changes, if necessary

In the end, you should have a routine that works best for you. No matter the case, following a set of systematic practices can help you become more organized, and successful. And don't get discouraged when things don't go as planned. Establishing a fixed routine takes time so be patient and don't give up.

# 8

# CONCLUSION ON HOW A DAILY ROUTINE CAN CHANGE YOUR LIFE?

———◦♭◦———

Our daily routine shapes our life. Most of our routines are habits controlled by the subconscious mind which has been programmed by the conscious mind. By making small changes in our daily routine, we can make huge changes in our life. By being conscious of our daily routine, we can program our subconscious mind. The subconscious mind performs our daily routines automatically. Your job is to reprogram your subconscious mind to do your daily routine to make your dreams into a reality

I would love to know your thoughts on how creating a daily routine works for you. I would be all ears to your feedback because I am eager to find ways to improve. I will listen to all your comments with an open mind and make an effort to fix your concern. Drop me an email on simbletashokan@gmail.com. I look forward to hearing from you.

# General Back matter

Dear Reader

I have Tried to keep this book error free. But if errors have crept in do let me know.

Thank you for buying this book

All trademarks and brands referred to in this book are for illustrative purposes only, are the property of their respective owners and not affiliated with this publication in any way. Any trademarks are being used without permission, and the publication of the trademark is not authorized by, associated with or sponsored by the trademark owner.